A Handyman's Guide

To Self –Publishing Your First Book

For Free

(or Almost Free)

Mike Woodcock

ISBN: 150300029X
ISBN-13: 978-1503000292

DEDICATION

This book is dedicated to my wife, whose idea for a book spurred my interest in non-traditional publishing, and to every person with a book in his or her head and an interest in seeing it in print..

CONTENTS

ACKNOWLEDGMENTS

I would like to thank my wife, Sherry, for being my muse, my editor, my friend and my biggest fan. I would like to acknowledge my children, Mara, Brittany, and Eric, who have taught me about loving and being loved. I would like to thank my dad for teaching me that hard work won't kill you. I would also like to acknowledge all of the authors who had ideas for books that never came to fruition. The thought that we are missing their influence in the world today because big publishing companies didn't think publishing their books would be profitable is not acceptable. We will only be able to heal the planet by sharing ideas freely, and by encouraging everyone to be a part of that process by finding their voices through writing and self-publishing.

CHAPTER 1- GETTING STARTED

How long have you wanted to write a book? Have you always had ideas that you wanted to share? Were you called to write? Most people carry the idea of writing a book with them for years. There is no research that I could find about the number of people who have a finished manuscript sitting in a box or saved in a file on their computer, or of those with an idea that they dream of turning into a book. But my guess is that there are probably hundreds of thousands of people around the world who have dreamed of writing a book. If you've ever been in a social setting and while talking to people mention that you've always wanted to write a book, the usual response is, "Yeah, me too!"

What's holding you and the other hundreds of thousands of people back? In the past, the traditional path to publishing has been to write your book, or have a good solid idea and then go out and try to sell it to a publisher. Whole markets have built up around this process. The book *The Writer's Market* has been a bestseller for years. If you wanted to sell your writing, then you bought *The Writer's Market* and started sending out inquiry letters to either publishers or agents. It was all very complicated and seemed pretty daunting and hopeless. What you may have thought is, "I can't." I am here to tell you that "You can!" Welcome to the brave new world of self-publishing!

Now, if you have the desire to write and be published you needn't be turned down by conventional publishers or ignored by agents. You, the author, have been put in control. If you have the talent, the desire, the motivation, the time, and some limited computer and internet skills, you can have your book published in e-book and in paperback, from edited manuscript to finished proof, in about a month's time. Now is the time for everyone who has dreamed of writing a book to take that step and live his dream.

This book is primarily written for the real do-it-yourselfer. There are companies out there who will publish your book as if it were self-published - meaning you continue to maintain control over most of the process: pricing, distribution, etc. Depending on how much money you are willing to part with, they will do most, if not all, of the heavy lifting.

My goal is that by the end of this book, you will be able to do it all yourself, and in the process save yourself a great deal of money. That being said, if you feel that your book will hit the bookshelves (both virtual and real) and immediately sell hundreds of thousands of copies, then you might want to let the publishing companies do all of the work. (We will talk a bit about the difference between costs and benefits of the various types of publishing later in the book.)

If you think you want to continue there's a bit of soul searching to do and some questions to answer.

TO DO: Look at the following questions and take time to make sure you have answered them. Why do I want this book published? Who is my audience? After reading my book, how will

their lives be enriched? What is the working title of my book?
What will the cover look like? How much time can I put in each
week toward publishing? After it's published, how much time can
I put in toward marketing?

Notes

_____

_____

_____

_____

_____

_____

_____

_____

_____

_____

_____

_____

_____

_____

_____

CHAPTER 2 - BEFORE YOU PUBLISH

OK, you've decided you're ready. (Wait a minute, go back and answer the questions in the previous section. I know you skipped ahead) Now what? There are some things to get in order before you publish. If you want anyone to read your book, you have to have an audience. By answering the previous questions you determined who your audience is. Now you have to determine ways to reach them. You need to create what some call your "author's platform." This is basically the framework or scaffolding that will support your marketing campaign after you have published your book. You are developing the market for your work before you release it. The best way to create this "presence" is to become an expert in your field or known by many in your niche or on the Internet. If you are a fiction writer you may have to develop your following by sharing your writing in small snippets in various forms. If you are writing nonfiction you also need to share your expertise in written form whenever and wherever you can. Those forms might include, but are not limited to, blogs (your own and guest blogging), articles, research articles, radio spots, interviews, and speaking engagements. We will address many of these more in depth later in the book.

Something else that needs to be in perfect order is your manuscript. Self-publishing has been a blessing and a curse. Because it is now possible to publish almost anything for almost nothing, there are many books published without ever being edited, and in some cases it seems like no one actually read the book before putting it into e-book format or even into print. Although your ideas may be truly divine ideas, unless you meticulously edit your book or have your book professionally edited, please consider whether or not the world needs one more poorly written, self-published book.

In the next part of the book, let's take a closer look at setting up your author platform, specifically, how to set up and maintain a positive presence on the Internet and how to use that presence to connect with prospective readers of your soon-to-be-published book.

Notes

_____

_____

_____

_____

_____

_____

_____

_____

_____

CHAPTER 3 - YOUR AUTHOR PLATFORM

The Internet is the perfect place for you to connect with like-minded people around the world and to use those connections to create future readers of your book. In order to do that you need to have access to a computer with internet and knowledge of, or a desire to learn about, blogging, Facebook and other social marketing platforms. Here are a few places you need to become familiar with: facebook.com; blogger.com; LInkedin.com; twitter.com; and youtube.com.

Let's start with Facebook. If you don't have a Facebook account it's easy to open one and get started. Visit facebook.com and sign up. If you already have a Facebook account, start creating a buzz about your upcoming book. You can create an author page by creating a page and selecting the Artist, Band, or Public Figure button. You can then choose Author in the drop down menu. That "page" will be your focal point on Facebook for your book and other writing. Visit your Facebook page and update with news and upcoming events.

If you like to write you should have your own blog. This is probably one of the most effective ways to create a fan base.

Ideally you would have started writing your blog before you focus on publishing your book, but as they say, "Better late than never." One of the easiest blogging platforms is Google's Blogger, at blogger.com. It's quick and simple to start your own blog. Don't worry about getting it just right; you can worry about changing the template and look later. Once you've begun, tell everyone, email your friends and associates. Invite them to visit you blog and share their comments. You want to generate "followers." Each follower is a prospective reader of your book.

The key to gaining followers is to write great content and be an active blogger. It is important that you post on your blog, but it is equally important to search out related blogs and then read and post comments. Some bloggers abuse this strategy of posting to other blogs; they simply direct the blog owner or other readers to visit their blog or website without contributing to the conversation. You want to add meaningful content to the blogosphere whenever you write, whether it's on your blog or on that of another blogger. Remember, you are creating a brand on the Internet. You don't want to be seen as a spammer, but a writer with insightful posts and comments. If new authors could focus on only one aspect of their author platform on the Internet, I would suggest focusing on creating an outstanding blog.

Another social media marketing outlet is Twitter. Twitter seems to be exploding in popularity. Started in 2006, it is reported that in 2011 Twitter hit over 100 million active users. On October 6, 2011, when Steve Jobs died, there were 6,049 tweets in one second. The estimated number of people registering on Twitter each day is in the hundreds of thousands. As Twitter continues to grow and change, more people will use Twitter as a means to keep in touch, much like text messages are used on phones.

Having said all of that, if you don't have a Twitter account you should set one up and use it as a means to keep in touch with your fans, updating as often as you can, adding quotes from your book, offering inspirational thoughts, or suggesting links to other meaningful information on the web.

Another powerful internet marketing tool is LinkedIn, at linkedin.com. According to Wikipedia, "LinkedIn is a business-related social network marketing site. Founded in December 2002 and launched in May 2003, it is mainly used for professional networking. As of August 4, 2011, LinkedIn reports more than 120 million registered users in more than 200 countries and territories." If you don't have an account, yes, you guessed it; set one up. Once it is set up, start inviting friends and associates and connect with as many people as you can. Within the network, there are "groups" that you join and each group has conversation threads that are started. When you first set up your account, search for groups that are related to your book. Join some groups and enter into an existing conversation or start your own. Remember that everything your write represents your brand, so you want to add to the conversation with meaningful comments.

In addition to the big boys of social networking, there are many smaller players. If you do an Internet search on "spiritual social networks" for example, you will find many smaller "niche" networks. These specific niche networks are not to be ignored. Search for these related social networks, join them and take part in the conversations. Make sure you spend some time on building your platform. Time spent in this endeavor will provide rewards later when you try to sell your book.

CHAPTER 4 - CREATING THE BUZZ

Your author platform is solid and you are now ready to start marketing your book. You may be saying, "I haven't even published my book yet. What do you mean market my book now?" Why do you think movie studios spend a great deal of money on previews of movies, usually well before they are released? They want to create interest by starting the buzz about their upcoming movie. Now it's your turn to begin marketing your book.

First, create a preview. The preview doesn't include the whole book. If you already have your book written, you may not want to include the title pages and table of contents. This is wasted space in the preview. You don't even need to include the first chapter, but do include your best work. This is your chance to hook your readers and sell your book. If you plan on using Createspace (which I encourage you to do), they have a free preview tool that allows you to upload a part of your book before it's published. Here's the link to the free preview tool: https://www.createspace.com/tools/preview.jsp

If you plan on using another option for publishing you will need to create your preview and save it for use in other places like your website and blog.

Now that you have your preview created, start creating the buzz by writing a post on your blog that shares your excitement about your soon-to-be-published book. In the blog post, tell the readers what they can expect from your book and when they might expect it. Use a picture of your book's cover to give them a visual. Even better, add a link to your preview so that your readers can read a bit of your book and get excited about what's to come. After writing about your upcoming book on your blog, make sure you announce it on your website, also adding a picture of your book's cover.

Blanket all of your social media. Make sure to post an announcement on your Facebook page about your upcoming book with a picture of your cover and a link to your preview. Ask your friends to share their comments about your preview. Tweet to all of your followers, making sure you have that link to your preview or your blog post. Post your announcement in all of your Linkedin groups, asking members to share their comments about your preview. If you are a member of any other niche social media, write an exciting announcement that your book is on its way.

Spend some time on this. I know that if you invest some time now, creating the buzz, your readers will be ready to snatch up your book once it's in print. I'm going to say it again. Don't skip this step! Spend some time marketing your book before you publish. You'll thank me later. Now you're almost ready to publish.

TO DO: Join as many social networks as you can. Start your Facebook author page. Create your blog and begin writing posts regularly and reading the blogs of people with similar interests. Follow their blogs and comment on their posts. Join Linkedin and join some writing groups to start posting and networking.

Notes

_____

_____

_____

_____

_____

_____

_____

_____

_____

_____

_____

_____

_____

_____

CHAPTER 5 - PUBLISHING OPTIONS

If you're reading this you are more than likely considering self-publishing. I do want to briefly describe other options that are out there. First, there is the traditional publishing route. If you are considering this there are six big players in the publishing business: Hachette Book Group, HarperCollins, Macmillan, Penguin Group, Random House, and Simon and Schuster.

In addition to the big six there are smaller publishing companies galore, with new companies springing up daily. If you want a quick glimpse of just how many publishing companies are out there and what they may typically publish, go down to your local book store and thumb through a copy of *Writer's Market*. Now also found online, *Writer's Market* was, and some say still is, the bible for writers wanting to publish books or have their articles published in print.

The first alternative to traditional publishing was what snooty authors and big publishers contemptuously called "vanity publishing." This type of publishing was reserved for authors whose work was not worthy of a traditional publisher, but used by authors who merely wanted to see their words in print.

Next up in publishing came a more "acceptable" method to getting your book published, self-publishing. Even the term self-publishing is somewhat ambiguous. There are also those who are taking a minimalist approach and taking their document to the local copy shops and having photocopies made, adding a simple cover and selling them themselves. Then there is POD or print-on-demand publishing. Services will vary with each company, and they may range from help with formatting and editing to just printing the print ready copy. These POD companies typically charge more for each copy.

In addition, there are what I call "assisted" self-publishing companies. The level of assistance differs depending on the amount of money you are willing to pay. As with traditional publishing, the number of "assisted" self-publishing companies is growing daily. To illustrate this growth, all you need to do is search the Internet for self-publishing companies.

There aren't the big six like there are with traditional publishing, but there are some big names that surface when you begin to look. At this point I want to insert a disclaimer: "Buyer beware." There are some good companies out there and some not-so-good ones. In this book I am not going to spend a great deal of space comparing the companies. What I will do is provide you with a list (see the appendix) that you can research and some websites that compare some of the more well-known self-publishing companies.

I think it is safe to say that non-traditional publishing is now firmly entrenched and here to stay. Those self-publishing pioneers may have been laughed at, but it seems the last laugh is on those who thumbed their noses at this type of publishing.

Within the last three years, getting your book in print via a non-traditional publishing approach outpaced traditional publishing. In general, the number of books printed each year is skyrocketing. Between 2002 and 2009, the number of books printed per year increased by 325%. In 2009 alone, according to Bowker, the world's leading provider of bibliographic information, the number of books published non-traditionally reached 764,448. With the exponential growth in non-traditional publishing, you can be one of those new, published authors.

Obviously those enormous stacks of books were not all best-sellers, but there were, without question, some great books printed by non-traditional publishing that otherwise may have never reached their readers.

Notes

_____

_____

_____

_____

_____

_____

_____

_____

_____

_____

CHAPTER 6 - SELLING BOOKS

You can't separate publishing from selling books. In the traditional business model, selling of books was highly dependent on the publisher. You wrote the book; they took all the risks, did all the marketing, covered all the costs and determined how and where your book would be sold. With the inception of Amazon, a new business model emerged for selling books. Amazon is arguably the Goliath of booksellers and has the ability to list millions of books for sale either, directly through Amazon or through one of their affiliates. Whereas publishers and brick and mortar book stores once determined the availability of books, now books can be made immediately available worldwide though the Amazon megastore. Hold on to that thought...

It's highly likely that most authors would like to sell their book. If the best-seller list is not your target, you would probably like to sell enough books to at least cover your costs. You may plan to use your book in conjunction with a workshop (like the plan for this book), or you may plan to have it be the first of a series of books. It may also be your life's goal to just get your book published. Regardless, I am going to assume you want to at least break even. That being the case, we should talk a little about royalties. Strictly and simply speaking, royalties are the net profit for the sale of a copy of your book. The royalties you receive from a traditional publisher (who covered all costs, did all the work, and took all the risks) will typically be between five and ten percent of the cover price on the book. That is a generality and oversimplifies the relationship between author and publisher. Each author enters into a contract with the publisher for each book that is written. For example, if your book had a $10 list price, you would earn between $.50 and $1.00 for each book. If you needed an agent to get your book published, his or her cut comes out of your profit. A typical agent may take ten to fifteen percent of your royalties. This is why the majority of writers have day jobs to support their writing habit!

Let's look now at non-traditional publishing. Selling books through non-traditional publishing will generate a bigger net profit per book. The size of that net profit depends on several variables that I will briefly explore next. First is the cost to print vs. the cost to purchase. That seems simple on the surface, but as you might expect, in publishing it's really more complicated. The cost to print in non-traditional companies varies. In this book I am going to illustrate one path to publishing through Createspace, but I want you to understand the differences in case you are dead set on choosing a different route.

How much does it cost to print a book? Many companies charge different prices depending on the number of copies ordered. The more copies you order, the cheaper the cost per copy will be. Thus, these companies with variable cost structures may be better if you know that you want to order 5,000 copies of your own book. Look into the fine print to determine if a variable printing cost better meets your needs. Some companies state that they have the lowest cost to print, but what I've discovered is that they make their money up somewhere else, like cover design, editing, or cost for additional distribution networks.

Cost to print is one factor in net profit; the other is how and through which distribution channels your book may be sold. For example, if I sell this book through Amazon I will receive a set percentage of the list price, but if I sell it through Createspace the percentage is higher. Even better, if I sell it through a workshop where I have the hard copy in hand, I make an even higher percentage. In fact, the net profit for a book sold from the hand of the author to the hand of the reader is the list price of the book minus the cost to print (plus shipping.) This is by far the highest profit margin for an author. There are other less obvious costs that should be considered, like the money and time spent on marketing (we'll talk more about this later.) Even still, this is the most profitable path for an author who may be targeting a specific niche.

Whatever route you choose to publish, the bottom line for net profit on a unit sold is the price of your book minus the total cost of producing that book.   The amount of money you will actually make selling a book that you have chosen to publish non-traditionally is directly related to the amount of time and effort you are willing to put in to marketing and distributing your book. Remember, in this case you are the publisher, agent, marketing team, head of public relations, bookstore manager, sales manager, and editor. The only thing you don't do is print the book (some die-hard authors actually go this route as well.)

CHAPTER 7 - LET'S REALLY GET STARTED

If you are still determined to write and are ready to fill all the positions mentioned in the previous chapter, let's get your book published! We'll start with an e-book. If you are serious about this writing thing and see yourself publishing more than this one book, there is some work that you can do to create a more substantial author's platform. (If you are not sure what an author platform is, go back and read the chapter titled "Your Author Platform.") Let's take a minute now to discuss publishing your book as an e-book first.

There is much chatter about e-books, and whether they will overtake the printed text. At this point e-books are not close to replacing books in print. That being said, there is still a market for e-books, and publishing a free e-book can be a strategy similar to what supermarkets do with what they call "loss leaders." The "loss leader" is an item priced very low, sometimes below cost, which brings customers in to the store. Once in the store, the belief is that a customer will buy other items, and that profit will cover the cost of the "loss leader" item. Investopedia.com explains this strategy, "The loss leader strategy is more than just a nifty business trick - It Is a successful strategy If executed properly."

I know this strategy works. My wife is a perfect example; she downloads free e-books and when she finds an author she likes, she downloads other books by the same author. And yes, she ends up buying additional books by the same author.

Whether you decide to publish a free e-book or not, the process will be the same. To publish your book, we are going to use one of the most popular and easy to use e-book publishing and distribution platform for e-book authors, Smashwords.

Notes

_____

_____

_____

_____

_____

_____

_____

_____

_____

_____

_____

CHAPTER 8 - MAKING A SMASH
WITH SMASHWORDS

Smashwords is not the only e-publishing company, but it's easy and it creates your e-book in many formats. Once you've published with Smashwords, you should also publish with Amazon Kindle Direct. By doing so, it will add your book to the Amazon library and get you into the Kindle Store. For now though, let's focus on Smashwords. (At the time of publishing this book, Amazon came out with a new program called Kindle Select. It is claiming to offer additional royalties **when you make your book exclusive to Kindle for at least 90 days. It will be part of the Kindle Owners' Lending Library for the same period and you will earn your share of a monthly fund when readers borrow your books from the library. You will also be able to promote your book as free for up to five days during these 90 days.** The downside is that for those 90 days you may not offer your e-book anywhere other than Kindle Direct.)

The first step to publishing with Smashwords is to join at smashwords.com. After registering you will set up your own My Smashwords page, where you will create a profile and add links to your blog or website. Once you're finished you are ready to publish your book. Before you upload your book you should read their **Style Guide**. The website claims that if you read and follow the Style Guide, the upload process will be painless. I agree completely; take the time to read it. It will ultimately save you time.

After reading their guide and editing your book for the final time, it's time to upload. Once you follow the link to publish your book, you will be asked to enter the following information: the title, a short description, a long description, the language in which the book is written, whether it has adult content, the price of the book, a category for your book, tags for your book, and the formats for your book. Then you will need to upload a cover image and select your file to upload. Once the above information has been added, all you need to do is click the Publish button.

Now let's get your book available at Amazon. First you need to create an account at **https://kdp.amazon.com**. Once the account is created you can add your book. Kindle Direct has it's own guidelines that you will find in their Kindle Publishing Guide found on the sign-in page under Getting Started & FAQs. Take the time to read through them. There are many helpful formatting tips that, if followed, will save you time in the long run. After you have created your account and read the guidelines, you can click the Bookshelf button and add your book by clicking the button called Start Your Title Now. Here is where you add all the information about your book as you did with Smashwords.

If your book is only to be offered as an e-book, skip to the Marketing Your Book section. If you want to also publish in print, continue reading.

CHAPTER 9 - CREATING A PRINT BOOK WITH CREATESPACE

The first step in getting your book to print is to join createspace.com. Follow the simple steps and once you have verified your account through your email, you are ready to create your book in print. The first decision you need to make is whether you are ready to do this yourself or need help. They will offer help from a consultant but remember, this is another way they make their money. If you're willing to do the work, I suggest doing it yourself.   The next step is to enter a working title and choose a setup process. I suggest using the "Guided" process.

Through the guided process you will be asked to add your working title, author's name, and a description and a subtitle. After completing this information you will need to secure an ISBN number.   There are several options available: you can have Createspace assign a free ISBN number; pay $10 for a custom ISBN that will allow you to publish with Amazon using your own imprint as the publisher, but not any other publisher; or you can purchase a custom universal ISBN for $99 which allows you to keep your distribution and publishing options open. If you already own an ISBN number you can use it as well. Once you've decided which ISBN option, you are ready to begin on the interior of your book.

Again, you have the option of having Createspace help with the design. Starting at $299, Createspace will help you design your book. If you choose this option a consultant will contact you. But because you are reading this book, I believe you will be able to do it yourself!

It's time to work on the interior of your book. There are some decisions that need to be made. First, is your book going to be black and white or color? The difference in price is a huge factor. The cost for a 150-page black-and-white book in a standard 6X9 format is $2.65 apiece. The cost for a full-color, 150-page, standard 6X9 format is..... $11.35! The point I'm trying to make is that if you feel full color pages are essential, you are going to have to charge a ridiculous price for your book to make any kind of profit. If you are only making the book for yourself or you want to only print a very small number of books for your friends, then perhaps full-color is an option. I would suggest for a first book, self-published, and from a yet-to-be-famous author, go with black and white with a nice full-color cover. Set the price of the book based on what other books of the same type might be selling for and keep the profit for yourself.

Next you need to upload your document. You can upload your work as a print-ready .pdf, .doc, .docx, or .rtf. Review the three helpful tips and ideas files at the bottom of the page: PDF Submission Guidelines, A Step-By-Step Guide to Formatting Your Book's Interior, and Creating a PDF for Print, before you upload. You may catch some errors that will save you time if corrected now.

Before you upload you should review your manuscript one last time. Check to make sure that the pages listed in your table of contents (if you have one) match up with the pages in the text of the book. Browse your computer for the file to upload and then choose that file.

Save the changes you have made by clicking save at the bottom of the page. Createspace will convert your text to PDF and it will run an automated print check to determine the final page count and check for any potential issues that might surface during printing. Once this process is complete you can check the issues with the "Interior Reviewer Tool."

It may take a while, so they give you an option to begin working on the cover of your book while you wait. Before you get to this step you should already have a cover designed and be ready to upload that in the next step.

You have several options to create your cover. You can build your own professional-quality book cover using your own photos, logos, and text. This handy tool automatically formats and sizes your cover based on your book's trim size and page count. You can have Createspace design your cover for a fee (starting at $149) or you can upload a print-ready PDF cover. Once again, Createspace has helpful tips and ideas at the bottom of the page.

As I mentioned earlier, you are reading this book because you know you can do this yourself. So, choose to build it yourself and let's get going! Using "Cover Creator" is relatively easy. You begin by choosing the design. There are five pages of designs. You can use one of their pictures for the cover or use your own. You can have a cover-ready image with title and author or, you can use an image and the Cover Creator will add the title and author name. This is where your creative genius gets to play. Remember that the cover is what helps to sell your book. A great cover will attract readers. If you are short on ideas, browse Amazon and look for covers that catch your attention and then ask yourself why.

Once you've played with Cover Creator, added your author photo, and created the back cover description, you are ready to upload the cover. Just click Upload the Cover. You are ready to submit your files and complete the setup. Once the files are submitted, Createspace will ensure your information complies with their submission requirements. You should receive an email within 48 hours with next steps. While you are waiting you can set up your distribution channels.

Distribution channels are where your books will be sold. Amazon used to charge $25 to distribute your books on "Expanded Channels," but now that is included. You will select both "Standard" and "Expanded" distribution channels.

I'm not sure why you have to select the "Expanded" channel, but it will increase the distribution of your book to bookstores, both online and brick and mortar, libraries, and certified retailers who can buy your book at a deeply discounted price.

Before they will let you choose your distribution channels, you will need to fill out your royalty payment profile. This will tell them where to send your royalty payments when they begin to amass.

The next step in the process is to set the price for your book. There are no hard and fast rules for pricing your book. As its publisher, this is completely up to you. For paperback fiction books the page count should be considered when pricing. For example, it's reasonable to ask $15.95 for a 350-page novel. Most average-sized paperback novels range from $12.95 to $17.95.

For nonfiction books, your book's price should be in line with books of similar size and subject matter. If there is a great deal of research, charts, graphs and illustrations, you may be able to set a higher retail price. Because you are self-publishing, you can choose to set your price on the lower end and still make a larger profit. Definitely spend some time looking around at Amazon.com and price yours comparably.

Now you can create your book's sales information, including description and an author biography. This information will be used in the sales channels you've chosen. You will need a description of your book in 4,000 characters or less. You will be asked for an author biography. Put some time into this, as you will need this for other promotional and marketing situations. Finally, you will need to determine the BISAC category. The Book Industry Standards and Communications (BISAC) categories are used by the book-selling industry to help identify and group books by their subject matter. This is where you are going to choose the BISAC category that best fits your book.

It's time to enter some search keywords. Search keywords can help your title show up on both amazon.com and search engines. Pick phrases that you think readers are likely to use when either searching for your title specifically, or when shopping for books that may be similar in subject matter.

You are now finished and all you need to do is wait. Within 48 hours you should receive an email from Createspace. If there are corrections that need to be made they will tell you at this time. If everything is fine you will now be able to move on to selling and marketing your book.

Notes

_____

_____

_____

_____

_____

_____

_____

_____

_____

_____

_____

_____

_____

_____

_____

_____

CHAPTER 10 - MARKETING YOUR BOOK

Up to this point things have been pretty easy; now begins the hard part. Once again, there are countless internet companies willing to take your money to do the marketing for you, but if you're reading this you probably want to keep your money for other things and do the heavy lifting yourself.

Before you begin you have some more questions to answer (do these now and you won't have to come back later.)

TO DO: Answer the following questions: What are you going to charge for your book? Have you written your author biography? Have you created a description of your book in 4,000 characters or less? What are some search keywords that readers might use when searching for your book or books like yours?

Now that you have answered the questions, let's go on. As with most endeavors, "Those who fail to plan, plan to fail." So, start with a good marketing plan. In order to execute your marketing plan you will need to create some marketing material. You've already written some of that material for Createspace. You will need to have a biography. You have to establish your audience. Who will read your books? You will need to determine your marketing goals and objectives: "By June I will sell 100 books by updating my blog weekly, participating in at least six forums, getting 10 reviews, five awards, and making three media appearances." You will need to determine where your book will be sold and you will need book descriptions.

Ultimately you may need several different descriptions, but to keep it simple we are going to focus on two, a short version and a longer version. You may have written a longer version for Createspace, but let's create a short version.

This short version should be 100 words or less. In these 100 words you want to tell the reader how reading your book will help them solve a problem or reach a goal. Here is a description that is 89 words.

> **A new book by Sherry Woodcock, *Learning to Forgive and Let Go*, looks at how simple spiritual tools can allow you to have more positive relationships and view circumstances, seen otherwise as negative, in a more positive light. Sherry explains how by allowing ourselves to let go of erroneous beliefs and negative feelings, we can live a more free and fulfilling life. "By forgiving and letting go of all the negative beliefs and feelings, I can imagine perfection unfolding and it is done. I can feel free and content."**

Readers want to know why they should spend the money to buy and take the time to read your books instead of some other author's book, and they will want to know a little bit about you.

So take some time to develop a short biography. There are no hard and fast rules about writing a short biography, but most agree it should be written in third person, be factual, contain any credentials or experience related to the topic of your book, and be interesting or capture the attention of the reader. Here is an example of my wife's bio.

> *Sherry Woodcock is a spiritual teacher, mother, grandmother, wife and author of Daily Spiritual Tools, the blog and the book. Sherry is on a life-long journey to find God in our daily lives. "If we are able to know God within ourselves, and as ourselves, in the midst of the day-to-day events of our lives, work, parenting, paying bills, doing our best and our not-so-best, we help to elevate others and our world."*

You can find may examples of author bios by doing an Internet search of "author bio examples."

Now that you have created a variety of marketing materials, including a short and long description of your book and your biography, you will need to get those materials in print on the internet and in hard copy.

TO DO: Write a description of your book. Write your author biography. Determine your audience. Create business cards. Develop marketing goals. Answer these questions: Where will you sell your book? What is your advertising budget? How can you leverage you social media presence to sell books? How can you use your web page and blog to market your book? What activities including book launches, book signings, and speaking engagements can you plan to promote your book?

CHAPTER 11 - YOUR MEDIA KIT

If you are self publishing you will probably *be* the marketing department. This means that you are now selling yourself. Get comfortable with it. You are the brand, not your book. If you plan on writing only one book, then you will be co-branding you and your book, but for the most part, you are the product. Authors I have met are not always the most extroverted individuals, and some are very uncomfortable seeing themselves as having something valuable to share. My belief is that there is a reader for every book written. You do have something to offer and now you need to let others know how they can enjoy your work. I've reviewed literally thousands of blogs, and seen that the biggest waste is a well-written blog that no one is reading. Marketing is the key, and for the author a good media kit is essential.

To begin building your media kit you will need to gather some of the material you have already created (If you haven't been creating as you go, you might want to consider that now.) You will also need to create some additional materials. You can start with the following: a description or synopsis of your book, your biography, high quality images of your book and yourself, information about how readers can find your book, and an interview with the author. Either interview yourself or ask a friend to interview you. The questions asked should provide information about the book or the process of writing the book. Ask yourself, what would a reader want to know? You can find examples of author interviews by doing an internet search for "author interview" to give you ideas.

In addition to the written interview, consider doing an interview either on Youtube or using an audio recording (see the appendix for resources for audio and video recording.) These are great to add on a website or blog.

You should also get reviews of your book. Sometimes you will have friends that will read and review your book. There are also companies and individuals that will read and review your book for a price. Some authors swear that professional reviews give your book more credibility. I'm not certain that's the case. If you know someone who may also be an expert in a field that is related to what you write about or if they themselves are published authors, you might encourage them to write a review or testimonial of your book. This review can serve two purposes - it can be included in your media kit or it can be included on the back cover of your book. Regardless, it is a valuable tool in your marketing toolbox.

If you've already published your book, it should be available in a variety of places on the Internet and hopefully in brick and mortar bookstores as well. If you published with Createspace you will automatically have a page generated with information about your book and a link to buy it. At the very least, list this page in the information in your media kit.

The images for your promotional material should be high quality and interesting. You may want to have different pictures of yourself including a headshot. This picture may also be the one you use on the back of your book. It should be obvious, but may need stating; use a picture that you want to represent you for years to come. Once this picture is on the back of your book or included in marketing material it is out there for good. Some authors will spend the money to have a professional photographer do the work, but if you are on a shoestring budget, make sure it's your best shot.

I would suggest having a picture of the cover of your book on all promotional material. I discovered an inexpensive way to get a great picture of my wife's book; I used Fiverr, http://fiverr.com. If you haven't heard of Fiverr, you are in for a treat. People around the world will do just about anything for five dollars. I had a three-dimensional picture made using the book cover jpeg. In fact the contractor made two different 3D images for only $5.00. I used it on flyers, posters, bookmarks, and postcards. What a bargain!

Your media kit should be available both online and as a printed set of materials. There are no hard and fast rules or even guidelines for how your material is organized or presented, but it is important that your material is organized and presented in a way that is easy to read and visually appealing.

You can create your promotional material on 8 ½ by 11 inch flyers or half sheet flyers, but you will also want to consider including items like business cards, postcards, bookmarks and posters.

You can and should create a press kit that includes all of the above. There are a variety of ways to present your material. This is where you get to be creative. One way you could present the press kit is to use one of those folders with pockets on both sides. Those can be found at your local office supply store. You can distribute the material in both sides of the folder with the eye-catching images above the pocket. This will encourage the reader to dig deeper into the information to find out more.

Because this material represents you and your book, you don't want to put off a prospective reader or a member of the press by presenting low-quality material. If you are printing your own material make sure it looks professional. You may want to spend a little here to have it printed professionally if your home printer isn't up to the job.

Some materials will have to be printed. There are many different companies that can print material like your business cards, post cards and posters. Most will require you to have print ready copy. Some companies will take your information and create the material for you; however, being the do-it-yourselfer, you will probably want to make your own. If that's the case you will need a good graphics program. I found Gimp, a free (I like free) program that will allow you to create your own graphics. I used it to create the cover for my wife's book and all the promotional copy for marketing. You can download it for free at http://gimp.org.

Once you've created the graphics or images you will use, you will have to create the various components of your media kit. I've found that there are quite a few online printers that enable you to design your own material online and order what you've designed. I used Zazzle, http://zazzle.com , for bookmarks, postcards, and posters. It's easy to use and the products are high quality. It may not be the cheapest online option, but with some searching you may be able to find a less expensive source.

TO DO: Consider these items for your media kit: a description of your book, your author biography, several author pictures, picture of your book, a list of where your book is available, interview questions, testimonials or reviews, flyers, postcards, and business cards.

Notes

_____

_____

_____

_____

_____

_____

_____

_____

_____

_____

_____

_____

_____

CHAPTER 12 - WHAT NOW?

So you have your book in one hand and your media kit in the other. You have a marketing plan, your author platform is created and you are beginning to create that buzz for your book. What do you do now? It's time to roll up your sleeves and get down to the business of getting your book into the hands of the readers and maybe selling a few copies (or a few thousand!)

Now's the time to really start working the social media - find every online group where members might be interested in your book and join the group. Facebook and Linkedin both have "groups" that are interest-specific. Join the groups and begin by "lurking" around. I know that sounds a little odd, but all that means is that you want to read what others are writing and get a feel for the group. Most groups will have posting guidelines. Make sure that when you post you adhere to these guidelines. No one likes a spammer. Once you feel you know the group (this might be hours or days) introduce yourself to the group.

A great group to start with at Linkedin is the Books and Writers group. It has, at the time of writing this book, over 33,000 members. Within the group there are a variety of discussion.

After lurking, find a discussion and join in. Introduce yourself, be real, add interesting comment, and mention your book and where people can find it. For Linkedin you want to build your network, so invite people to join your network when it seems appropriate.

Facebook is another monolith of social media. Take time to find and join groups on Facebook by using the search feature. Join a few groups that may contain members who may read your book and start "lurking" again. Once you've become familiar with the group, join in the conversation by introducing yourself and your book. Remember these are social networks. People come for the relationships. Once you have established yourself as a trusted source of interesting information, then members may be interested in looking at your book. On Facebook you want to build your "friend" base in order to spread the word about your book.

Twitter is yet another opportunity in social media. This can start to feel overwhelming, but if you focus on maybe three of the big social media networks, this will begin to build your fan base. As with every other form of Internet "marketing," there are three major factors that can create a huge success or a dismal failure: content, content, and content. Even with the tiny tweets (only 140 characters), if what you send out to the virtual world is not worth reading, this will create the belief that whatever you write is not worth reading. Tweet the announcement of your book, tweet when you have an event, tweet announcements of new features to your website, or quotes from your book or blog.

Whatever social media you choose to use, it is important to be active. This doesn't mean that you have to tweet every thought you have or tell your fans what you are having for breakfast, but it means that you keep current and interact. Interaction is not waiting for someone to respond to what you have written, but reading what others have written and responding in a thoughtful way. You need to make sure that you screen your interactions. What I mean is that not everyone will be an asset to your marketing plan. For example, a person who has thousands and thousands of followers on Twitter, but is an online "marketing guru," will probably not respond to anything you tweet directing him or her to visit your blog to read your latest post. A better prospect on Twitter is someone who has followers numbering in the hundreds. It's more likely that they actually read what you tweet and may visit your website and become a reader of your book in addition to following you on Twitter.

When someone wants to "friend" you on Facebook or begins to follow you on Twitter, you will get an email notification. This is where the door is ajar. You now have an opportunity to reel them in to read some of what you have written. People on the Internet are looking for content that is well written (I mentioned that before), but is also of interest to them. So you need to craft a "Thank You" for the friend invite or the "follow" on Twitter. Every time you write something and it's going to be posted on the Internet you need to create an invitation in some form or fashion. You are inviting them to either sample your book, read a blog post, download the e-book, or to get more information. You can just invite them to visit your website, but if you do you need to tell them why. Here are a couple of examples.

> *Thanks for the friend invitation. It's nice to connect with like-minded spirits. I'm a writer and author of Daily Spiritual Tools, the book and the blog. I'd love it if you stopped by and shared your ideas on my blog.*
> *http://dailyspiritualtools.blogspot.com (This directs the new*

friend to her blog to share ideas.)

Thanks for following Daily Spiritual Tools. Download my new e-book "Learning to Forgive and Let Go" for $0.99 http://tinyurl.com/7wp8deh (This takes the follower to the Amazon page to buy the book, with a shortened URL.)

Thanks for following Daily Spiritual Tools. Please visit my website to read my blog and book. Http://dailyspritualtools.com (This invites the follower to her website to read the blog and book.)

With the door ajar you will have only a short time and a small space to invite them to be your next reader and avid fan. For Twitter, when you get the "new follower" notification, you will then visit the profile of the follower and tweet your "Thank You" to them. You will have only 140 characters, including their Twitter name, to create your invitation. With Linkedin you can send messages directly to members of your network and the text is not limited. I would use this judiciously; the people on Linkedin tend to be professionals and don't appreciate spam-like, impersonal communication.

Another successful strategy when using groups in social media is to offer a "special offer" for members of the group only. With Createspace and Smashwords you can create coupons or discounts with special discount codes that have an expiration date attached. This is another way to build your fan base.

SOCIAL MEDIA TIPS AND TRICKS

1. Set up a signature with your book title, web and/or blog address, and an address where someone could buy your book.
2. Sell yourself, not your book.

3. Schedule 30 minutes, several times a week to interact on your social media.

4. Schedule one longer session weekly to create content that you can use during the week.

5. Create a document with pre-written responses to "friend" or network invitations that are network specific.

Notes

_____

_____

_____

_____

_____

_____

_____

_____

_____

_____

_____

_____

CHAPTER 13 - STEP AWAY FROM THE COMPUTER

So far you have spent a great deal of time sitting in front of your computer. If you paid attention earlier in the book you should have already been hitting the streets and building your author platform by speaking to people about your book or the subject of your book. If you wrote a nonfiction book, you want the public to view you as an expert. If your book is fiction, you want people to get to know you and subsequently want to learn more about you by buying your book.

There are many opportunities for speaking engagements, but you will need to put in some legwork to create them. First, most larger cities have a community center where classes are offered. Look it up and find out what you have to do to offer a class. Next, many community service clubs are looking for speakers. Get involved in a club that interests you and find out how to volunteer to speak. Also, larger cities and some libraries have a speakers' bureau that may take volunteers to add to their lists. Talk to friends and family members and let them know that you would be happy to come to speak to any group about your book or subject matter. As with everything already mentioned, before you speak to anyone you should know exactly what you are going to say.

Practice your presentation, be professional no matter the size or type of group to whom you are speaking, and have copies of your book available for purchase at the event.

Another way to get out there is to plan an event around the launch of your book (aptly called a book launch) or plan events after your launch where you can talk about your book and sign copies for those who purchase your book. Remember, these events are the bread and butter of the self-published author. You make the largest profit on books you sell directly from your hand to the hand of the reader.

First, find a venue for your event. Many times a bookstore or library will allow you to have an event there. Next, work out the scheduling arrangements and event details with whomever will be hosting your event. Then, create all of the promotional materials well ahead of the planned event. Promote the heck out of the event. This means contacting everyone, friends, family, old friends, all social network contacts, the local media, and whoever will allow you to put a flyer in their window. This is not the time to be shy or worry that you are bugging people. This is the time to blanket your area with news of your event. Use materials you created for your media kit earlier in the book.

I would also suggest that you write a press release that you can share with the local paper, radio or TV station. This is an important part of your media blitz, but you can write it yourself using good writing skills (which you possess) and a standard format.

PRESS RELEASE GUIDELINES

1. Use the title to catch the reader's attention and foreshadow what follows.

2. Make your release newsworthy. Why should someone bother reading it?

3. Make sure your lead paragraph answers who, what, when, where, and why?

4. Use good writing, an active voice and strong verbs.

5. Keep it short, one page of no more than 250 words.

6. Use standard press release format (see the appendix for format and examples.)

Notes

_____

_____

_____

_____

_____

_____

_____

_____

_____

_____

CHAPTER 14 - IS THIS THE END OR JUST THE BEGINNING?

We find ourselves at the end of this book. Depending on how many times you started and stopped, it may have taken you a day to read the book or it may have taken a month. Regardless, if you finished the book and if you have any determination to publish your own book, know that you can publish it yourself. This may not be the easiest process or guarantee success, but depending on how you measure success, just completing the book from idea to published manuscript is quite the accomplishment. You will see your book published if you follow this simple handbook on self-publishing.

I hope that this book has been a useful tool and that your first experience in self-publishing is just that - your first experience, with many to follow. May your days be filled with the wonders of life and ample opportunities to pursue your passion of writing and sharing your ideas.

In the following appendix you will find useful resources and examples that will help you along your self-publishing journey.

APPENDIX I

SELF-PUBLISHERS AND PRINT ON DEMAND PUBLISHERS

48 Hour Books http://www.48hrbooks.com/

A&A Printing http://www.printshopcentral.com/

Adv Advantage Medina Group http://www.amgbook.com/

Angel Printing http://www.angelprint.com/

Apex Book Manufacturing http://www.apexbm.com/

Art Book Bindery http://www.artbookbindery.com/

Authorhouse http://www.authorhouse.com/

Aventine Press http://www.aventinepress.com/

Blitz Print Inc. http://www.blitzprint.com/

Blurb http://www.blurb.com/

Book Blocks http://www.bookblocks.com/

Book Stand Publishing http://www.e-bookstand.com/

Booklocker http://www.booklocker.com/

Booksurge http://www.booksurge.com/

Createspace http://www.createspace.com/

Dorrance Publishing http://www.dorrancepublishing.com

Equilibrium http://www.equilibriumbooks.com/

Foremost Press http://foremostpress.com/

Infinity Publishing http://www.infinitypublishing.com/

Inkwater Press http://www.inkwaterpress.com/

Instant Publisher http://www.instantpublisher.com

iuniverse http://www.iuniverse.com/

Llumina http://www.llumina.com/

Lulu http://www.lulu.com/us/en

Magic Valley Publishing http://www.magicvalleypub.com/

Mill City Press http://www.millcitypress.net/

Morris Publishing http://www.morrispublishing.com/

Outskirts Press http://www.outskirtspress.com/

Omega Publishing http://www.omegapublications.net/

Publish America http://www.publishamerica.com

SelfPublishing.com http://selfpublishing.com

Trafford http://www.trafford.com/

Universal Publishers http://www.universal-publishers.com/

Virtual Bookworm http://www.virtualbookworm.com/

Wasteland Press http://www.wastelandpress.net

Wheatmark http://www.wheatmark.com/

Wing Span http://www.wingspanpress.com/

Wordclay http://www.wordclay.com/

Wordpro Press http://wordpro.com/press/

Xlibris http://www2.xlibris.com/

Xulon Press http://www.xulonpress.co

APPENDIX II

PRESS RELEASE STANDARD FORMAT

Use 8 1/2" x 11" white paper with 1" margins.

Use a font like Courier or Times.

In the upper left corner in capital letters write FOR IMMEDIATE RELEASE:

Double space and give your name and **all** contact information, including how to reach you in the evening at home. Do you have an address, home and office telephone numbers, a fax number, an email address, and a web site? Include them all.

Two lines down type your headline in **boldface.** Capitalize the first letter of each word except for *a, an, the, of, to,* and *from.*

Two lines down from the headline, type in your city and the date you are sending the press release. Follow immediately on the same line with the body of your press release.

At the end, in point form, recap details of your book's release date or your book signing or whatever you are announcing.

Use only one side of the paper, which should not be a problem if you have kept your word count down.

THE LAST LINE IS THREE ###S CENTERED

SAMPLE PRESS RELEASE (BORROWED FROM CREATESPACE)

FOR IMMEDIATE RELEASE

Author Shares Story of Finding Spirituality in Unexpected Places

Carol Gino helps readers explore their own Inner Knowing in "There's an Angel in my Computer: A Journey of Spiritual Emergence"

AMITYVILLE, New York (MMD Newswire) October 25, 2011 -- In this groundbreaking new book, Carol Gino explores the importance of expanded awareness in preparing for the New World Consciousness of 2012. "It may not be the end of the world," she says, "but it certainly is the end of the world as we know it."

Carol Gino spent much of her life searching for a vision of the Divine. In the spiritual self-help book, "There's an Angel in my Computer: A Journey of Spiritual Emergence" (ISBN 1936530007), Gino shares her quest and shows how her prayers were answered.

Gino finds the divine in the strangest of places. Through her journey, readers get the opportunity to explore the dance between spirit and soul. Readers witness Gino's personal transformation. Due to these changes, Gino discovers new aspects of herself. As she learns to recognize the voice of her own soul, she is able to reinvent herself and reframe the reality in which she lives.

"With the shadow of fear looming in connection with the 2012 prophecies - and so much terror projected in the media, I believe this is the best time to introduce a dialogue between the spirit and soul which is lighter and more playful. One in which life, in its greatest potential, is an adventure and an exploration of the best of human nature." Gino says.

"There's an Angel in my Computer: A Journey of Spiritual Emergence" is available for sale online in paperback and e-book formats on her website and at Amazon.com and other channels.

MEDIA CONTACT:

Carol Gino

Email: staff@starwater.com

Phone: (512) 718-4221

Website: http://rashanasmagicgarden.com

REVIEW COPIES AND INTERVIEWS AVAILABLE

###

APPENDIX IV

RESOURCES FOR AUTHORS

Audio Pal http://www.audiopal.com/

AudioPal is an amazingly simple, FREE, web application for recording 60 second audio blog posts. Great little embedded audio player is immediately emailed to you and within minutes place on your blog or website. Pretty cool for adding interactive marketing to your site.

The Authors Show
http://www.wnbnetworkwest.com/WnbAuthorsShow.htm
l

The Authors Show is not a "show" in the traditional sense of the word, it is a professional book marketing audio & video program. Radio interviews and the original broadcast are done at no cost. Interview copies and/or archiving of interviews for periodic rerun on the show are available for a nominal fee.

Audacity http://audacity.sourceforge.net/

Audacity is a free tool for recording and editing audio, great for creating audio recordings of your book to be added to Youtube videos

Gimp http://www.gimp.org/

Gimp is a great free graphic design tool for creating amazing book covers

Zazzle http://www.zazzle.com/

Zazzle is a great place to create book marketing tools like posters, post cards, and bookmarks- good quality

DanOSongs http://www.danosongs.com/#music

Royalty free great music easy to use on book trailers or podcasts

Smashwords http://www.smashwords.com/

This is an easy to use online e-book publishing site. Get your book in e-book format following their style guide and immediately upload for sale on major online book stores.

CreateSpace https://www.createspace.com/

Self publishing arm of Amazon, easy to use and immediately gets your book on Amazon.

Hootsuite http://hootsuite.com

This is a great website that allows you to manage all of your social media from one place. You can schedule and send messages to all of your favorite social networks like Face-book, Twitter, Linkedin and many more. This is an amazing time saver.

ABOUT THE AUTHOR

After spending over 30 years in public education as a teacher and school principal Mike Woodcock was challenged one day with helping his wife follow her dream of writing and publishing a book. Following the idea that necessity is the mother of invention, knowing that his wife wanted to self-publish her book, he researched the best strategies for self publishing and with this knowledge, helped her publish her first book, Daily Spiritual Tools and three more e-books so far. This experience sparked an interest in, and enthusiasm for, helping others fulfill their dreams of publishing their own book. Mike looks forward to spending his days split between hiking and backpacking the Sierras, following his own spiritual practice, and traveling the world sharing his self-publishing insights and strategies. To read more by Mike Woodcock visit his blog, Yes You Can Publish for Free at http://publishfree.wordpress.com

www.ingramcontent.com/pod-product-compliance
Lightning Source LLC
Chambersburg PA
CBHW070614290526
45790CB00002B/917